John Romita, Sr.
Artist

by Sue Hamilton

Visit us at
www.abdopublishing.com

Published by ABDO Publishing Company, 4940 Viking Drive, Suite 622, Edina, Minnesota 55435.
Copyright ©2007 by Abdo Consulting Group, Inc. International copyrights reserved in all countries.
No part of this book may be reproduced in any form without written permission from the publisher.
ABDO & Daughters™ is a trademark and logo of ABDO Publishing Company.

Printed in the United States.

Editor: John Hamilton
Graphic Design: Sue Hamilton
Cover Design: Neil Klinepier
Cover Illustration: Courtesy John Romita
Interior Photos and Illustrations: pp 1–32: All Marvel comic book character and cover images used
with permission by Marvel Entertainment, Inc.
Photos of John Romita, his family, and artwork, courtesy John Romita, pp 1, 7, 9-11, 16, 26.
p 5 John Romita, Corbis.
p 14 Stan Lee, AP/Wide World.
p 17 *Secret Hearts* and *Girls' Love* covers, courtesy DC Comics.
p 29 John Romita, Joe Sinnott, and Stan Lee, courtesy of the Joe Sinnott family.

Library of Congress Cataloging-in-Publication Data

Hamilton, Sue L., 1959-
  John Romita, Sr. / Sue Hamilton.
    p. cm. -- (Comic book creators)
  Includes bibliographical references and index.
  ISBN-13: 978-1-59928-302-9
  ISBN-10: 1-59928-302-6
 1. Romita, John--Juvenile literature. 2. Cartoonists--United States--Biography--Juvenile literature.
I. Title. II. Series: Hamilton, Sue L., 1959- Comic book creators.

PN6727.R637Z63 2006
741.5092--dc22
  [B]
                        2006015406

Contents

"Jazzy" John Romita 4

Start in Art 8

The Korean War 10

Bad Times for Comics 12

Eight Long Years 16

Back in Action 18

The Amazing Spider-Man 20

Fantastic Four 22

Special Projects 24

In the Family 26

Still Helping People 28

Glossary 30

Index 32

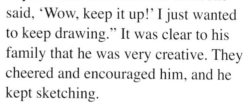

"Jazzy" John Romita

Working as a Marvel artist, John Romita, Sr., drew some of the most famous comics of all time, including *The Amazing Spider-Man, Fantastic Four, Daredevil,* and *Captain America.* "Jazzy" John Romita always worried that he had to catch up to the more experienced staff artists. But in fact, his beautiful drawings of heroic characters, plus his amazing method of "jazzing" up dull pictures, made John Romita one of the top comic book artists of the 20th century.

John V. Romita was born January 24, 1930, in Brooklyn, New York, to Victor and Marie Romita. John was the oldest of five kids. His three sisters and brother could all sing and dance, but not John. His talent lay elsewhere. Said John, "I began drawing when I was five years old. The first time someone said, 'Wow, keep it up!' I just wanted to keep drawing." It was clear to his family that he was very creative. They cheered and encouraged him, and he kept sketching.

By the time John was eight years old, he began reading comic books, which had recently become very popular. In 1938, John bought two copies of the first Superman comic ever published, *Action Comics #1.* He kept one copy clean and safe in a bag. He traced the other, learning how the action and story went together.

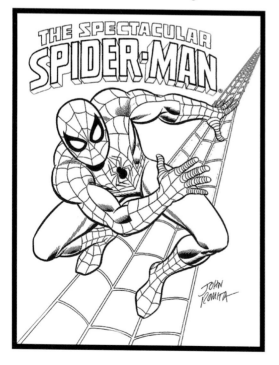

Left: Original Spider-Man art, drawn by John Romita.

Above: The talented "Jazzy" John Romita created amazing, fantastic comic books for over 50 years.

Above: John Romita studied Milton Caniff's *Terry and the Pirates* to understand how comics were created.

Other kids thought there was some kind of mechanical trick to making comic pictures. None of them thought that someone actually drew every single panel in a comic book. But John knew that artists created the comic books. He studied the style of comic artists, from Joe Simon and Jack Kirby's *Captain America* to Milton Caniff's newspaper comic strip, *Terry and the Pirates*. John began to understand how comics came together and what made them great.

John couldn't afford to buy chalk, so he sometimes created street art using chunks of plaster from torn-down buildings. When he was 10, he drew the Statue of Liberty on a street near his Brooklyn home. This was no ordinary drawing: it was a 100-foot (30-m) long Lady Liberty, running from one manhole cover to the next, two-thirds the size of the real thing! People came from blocks away, hoping to see the drawing before rain washed it away. When the rain did come, John had a clean slate to start drawing again.

John's artistic ability was also recognized in his school. He was asked to paint backgrounds and scenery for plays. He created murals on wrapping paper along entire school corridors. Even then, his work was very popular.

When John reached high school age, he wanted to learn better use of his art skills. His mother gave him permission to go to the School of Industrial Art (SIA), founded in 1936 in New York City. John's father didn't think his son would be able to make a living as an artist. Other people made John question his talent, as well. John recalled, "I was the third best artist in my class. There were two guys that were far superior to me. The second best artist came up to me and said, 'John, you really shouldn't do this. You aren't good enough.'"

But John's mother believed he was talented enough to make it work, and John proved her right when a chance meeting with a friend started him on his ultimate career.

Above: John Romita, age 15, with his mother, Marie, and father, Victor.

Start in Art

In high school, John wanted to study cartooning, but the class was too small—only three people signed up. He and the others found themselves placed with book illustrators. He studied magazine illustration, and loved the full-color images found in the popular *Saturday Evening Post* and *Collier's* magazines. He began to think that maybe he wanted to be a magazine illustrator, but that's not where his art took him.

When John graduated from high school in 1947, he began working as a commercial artist. He performed minor corrections, called touch-ups, on the illustrations of such major clients as Coca-Cola.

One day while on a train, John had a chance meeting with Lester Zakarin, an artist friend and fellow SIA graduate. Lester told John that he was working for Stan Lee, who was an editor at Timely Comics (which would later be known as Atlas Comics, before finally taking the name Marvel Comics). Lester was making good money, but he wasn't a good penciller, someone who used a pencil to sketch rough drawings. Instead, Lester was a skilled inker. An inker used black ink to make clear, clean black outlines over rough pencil lines, which created the final art. Lester was expected to do both jobs, but he could not easily draw the initial pictures. So, since most comic book artists worked at home or from their own office space, he secretly enlisted the help of John Romita.

John penciled the comics and Lester inked them. Then Lester turned in the entire finished product as his own. Both John and Lester made good money. However, Lester discovered that it was difficult to lie and not get caught.

Once, after Lester had presented a "finished" comic to Stan Lee, the perfectionist editor asked for a correction. Lester couldn't do the work himself. He had to think fast.

Below: The cover of *Strange Tales* #3. Inside the issue, John Romita penciled the story, "The Man Who Never Was," even though Lester Zakarin took the credit.

Left: Romita's future wife, Virginia, visiting John while he was stationed at Fort Dix, New Jersey, in 1951.

Lester made an excuse that he needed to work alone. He arranged to meet Romita at the New York Public Library, which was near the Timely Comics offices on the 14th floor of the Empire State Building. John penciled the correction. Lester inked it and returned to Timely with the newly revised artwork.

For over a year, John penciled the stories, while Lester did the inking and took credit for creating the entire comic book. John discovered that it was difficult to allow another person to take credit for his work. Plus, he had begun to get serious about a young lady named Virginia, and if he wanted to get married, he needed to have his own career.

John decided that he would soon tell Stan Lee that he was the one doing the penciling. But then, the Korean War changed John's plans.

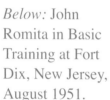

The Korean War

The war between North and South Korea began in June 1950. The United States was an ally of South Korea. John was drafted to serve in the Korean War in the spring of 1951.

Before reporting for duty, John learned from a friend about an artist job in a division that created military recruiting posters. Another soldier was leaving the position, and John wanted his job.

Romita showed his artwork to an Air Force captain, who was the art director at Governor's Island in New York Harbor. Much to the relief of John's family members, who feared that he would have to fight, John ended up being assigned to Governor's Island in the fall of 1951.

It was after joining the service that John decided to do something about his career. Since he was allowed to leave the military base from time to time, John went to see Stan Lee.

John went to the Timely Comics offices and told Stan's secretary that he was the one doing the pencil work for Lester Zakarin. She went in to Stan's office, and then came out with a horror script for John to pencil *and* ink. Well, John didn't think he was a very good inker, but he didn't want to tell them that. He wound up doing the whole job. He was now a full-fledged artist working on comic books, even though he was in the service at the same time.

Below: John Romita in Basic Training at Fort Dix, New Jersey, August 1951.

Left: John and Virginia Romita, on the day of their wedding, November 9, 1952.

For more than a year and a half, John kept working on recruiting materials. It wasn't the most challenging or exciting job, but he was safe, and his family was very thankful for that.

During this time, John and Virginia decided to start their lives together. The two were married on November 9, 1952. John was still in the service, but he continued to keep busy working on comic books in his off-duty time.

In July 1953, the Korean War ended, and John was about to be discharged. Just as a friend had helped Romita get into the division working on posters, John did a good deed for another friend.

John had been promoted to staff sergeant. An artist friend, Carmine Infantino, wanted his brother, Jimmy, who had been drafted, to take John's place. John got Carmine's brother into the same regiment on Governor's Island. Carmine, who was a successful comic book artist himself, was so grateful that he recommended John to the editors of DC Comics, as well as contacting Stan Lee. Of course, Stan already knew that John was terrific, having kept John busy nearly the entire time that Romita was in the service!

In 1953, John was now a professional comic book artist. He was working for DC and Atlas Comics (Timely's latest name). He and Virginia welcomed a son, Victor, in November of that year. Things seemed good, but he, and everyone else in the comic book business, would soon face some very difficult times.

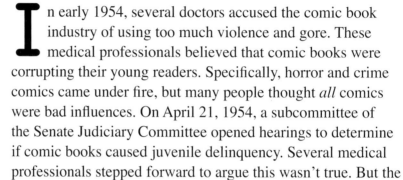

Bad Times for Comics

In early 1954, several doctors accused the comic book industry of using too much violence and gore. These medical professionals believed that comic books were corrupting their young readers. Specifically, horror and crime comics came under fire, but many people thought *all* comics were bad influences. On April 21, 1954, a subcommittee of the Senate Judiciary Committee opened hearings to determine if comic books caused juvenile delinquency. Several medical professionals stepped forward to argue this wasn't true. But the damage to the comic book business had been done. Parents believed that comics were bad, and that resulted in a huge decrease in sales.

John began to think that the comic book industry was dead. To him, the industry had been a stepping stone. He planned to work in comics long enough to get some money in the bank, and to become a better illustrator. He warned his wife Virginia that he might be out of a job soon.

Left: Many horror and crime comic books of the early 1950s, such as *Astonishing* #27, alarmed parents and children's groups because of their lurid and often graphic depictions of violence and gore.

Many people did lose their jobs. To stop the death of the industry, comic book publishers created the Comics Magazine Association of America. They agreed to follow the 1954 Comics Code Authority, which called for all comic books to follow specific rules about what subjects were allowed. Comics could then display a seal of approval on their covers. Many people thought this was censorship and violated the First Amendment, the right of free speech. But members of the comic book industry felt they had to agree to this to stay in business.

Above: Dr. Fredric Wertham, author of *Seduction of the Innocent*, was a vocal critic of violent comic books.

Above: Marvel Comics writer, creator, and editor, Stan Lee, in 2002. Early in John Romita's career, another artist, Carmine Infantino, thought he was helping Romita get work when he went to Stan Lee encouraging the editor to hire John. But Stan said, "You don't have to beg me to give work to John Romita; I'll give him all the work he wants!" Although there were some rough years, Stan kept his promise.

Still, many publishers and printers went out of business. The distributors, who sent the comic books to stores across the country to be sold, went out of business as well. Artists, writers, inkers, colorists, and letterers were suddenly unemployed. It was a horrible time to be in comics.

Luckily, John continued working. He wondered if he should try harder to become a commercial illustrator, but he enjoyed working on comic books. He continued to learn and study the techniques of other artists. He often felt that as the "youngster," he was trying to catch up. However, Romita had a unique style, and developed a beautiful shading technique. When he turned in his first pages using this style, Stan Lee loved it. The editor wanted other artists to use John's art technique.

Comic book artists were paid by the page. To get their work done, and make a decent amount of money, they had to be fast. John's technique, while beautiful, took too much time. When Stan asked other artists to copy Romita's style, there were quite a few upset artists. Luckily, it became clear that this wouldn't work with a comic book's tight deadlines. Even John was glad to eventually go back to a simpler style.

While John improved his art, the comic book industry continued to have difficulties. In 1958, Marvel Comics hit bottom. John earned $44 per page when things were going well. After 1954, his payment rates from Marvel started dropping until he was down to $24 per page. Finally, Stan Lee was ordered by Martin Goodman, the owner of the company, to let a number of artists go, keeping only a few to work on the best-selling comic books. John was one of those who lost his job. He turned to another industry leader, DC Comics, and found "romance."

Eight Long Years

In 1958, John Romita went to DC Comics, looking for work. Although he had a great deal of experience, neither the superhero nor the Western comic book editors needed another artist. However, the romance division wanted his skills.

John had worked on romance books in the early 1950s, but dropped that work to concentrate on action-oriented comics. Suddenly, he found he had a slight problem.

Having spent so much time working on comics with few women, Romita needed to learn to draw ladies and draw them well. His friend, fellow artist Carmine Infantino, helped him out. John said, "He showed me how to draw women. He said I was doing too lumpy a silhouette, and he was right. He said you need to get a very compact, simple silhouette, and put the details inside."

John was a quick learner, and found himself working on such titles as *Secret Hearts, Falling in Love,* and *Girls' Love Stories.* There were beautiful ladies, handsome men, lots of kisses and tears, but not very much in the way of exciting action and adventure.

But John had a family to support. He really needed a steady job, and he kept working despite the boredom. For eight long years, John attempted to create art with personality. He wanted to bring some of his style into the romance comic book pages. But, as he once said, "The normal romance is very bland." There wasn't a lot for him to do with these books, whose stories were very similar from month to month.

Below: John and Virginia Romita, with sons Victor and John, Jr., in 1962.

Although dull, working on romance comics gave him a new edge: he had to make something out of a simple story. Forcing himself to "jazz up" the romance comics, he became a better artist. If the story required the girl to sit staring lovingly at a guy, nothing much was happening in that panel. John added flowing hair, blowing leaves, a curtain twisting in the wind, anything to add some action. He used imaginative angles for the characters, twisting and turning bodies in different ways. All of this added up to training that would eventually lead him back to Marvel Comics and Stan Lee.

Above: Covers of romance comic books drawn by John Romita. John worked on hundreds of romance titles for DC Comics, until one day the company decided they had enough. After eight years, John was told that his services were no longer needed. Rather than sending John to another department, he was let go. DC's error became Marvel Comics' gain. A few weeks later, DC did try to get John back, but by then he had agreed to work for Stan Lee at Marvel. So began John Romita's decades-long employment with Marvel Comics.

Back in Action

I n 1966, although John was an excellent worker, DC Comics decided they had enough romance. After eight long years, they said good-bye to Romita. Once again, he was out looking for work. John called Stan Lee, and soon Romita was back working at Marvel Comics.

John was tired of penciling, and just wanted to do some inking. Stan started him inking another artist's pages of *The Avengers*. However, when Stan had a page with problems, he turned to Romita for help. John redrew the page and just like that, he was back being a penciller.

Below: Two Romita-drawn *Daredevil* covers.

John's next assignment was to work on a new comic book, *Daredevil, The Man Without Fear.* Created by Stan Lee and Bill Everett, this blind character, named Matthew Michael Murdock, was one of the the first handicapped superheroes.

Several top Marvel artists worked on the initial issues, but John began his work on *Daredevil* in 1966, using his own stylized deep shadows and clear bone structure. The only problem was, when Stan looked at the final version, there were several pages that didn't work. He thought the pace was "too slow." Stan called in one of John's heroes, Jack "King" Kirby, who did a "page breakdown." Basically, Jack did the simplest of outlines for the story, showing how the story should be "paced." John took that, learned from it, and from then on, was on his own.

Meantime, a DC editor contacted him to work on Metamorpho, the Element Man, a character who was able to alter both the chemical composition and the shape of his body. But John had agreed to do *Daredevil* for Stan Lee and turned down the DC work. John stuck by his word to Stan, plus he was more than a little mad at how DC had treated him. Later, John would wonder what would have happened had he gone back to DC at that time. Would he have worked on Superman or Batman?

But John was back in the "bullpen," Marvel's name for their group of staff artists. Stan Lee, known for his crazy nicknames, dubbed him "Jazzy Johnny" Romita. However, a major change was about to happen at work to draw John even further into Marvel's web.

Left: Daredevil, created by Stan Lee and Bill Everett, was a superhero with a handicap. John Romita started drawing the blind character in 1966. The covers at left are an example of Romita's stylized deep shadows and clear bone structure.

The Amazing Spider-Man

Only a few weeks after coming back to Marvel, John found out that Steve Ditko, the artist who had co-created Spider-Man, the company's number-two-selling comic, had decided to leave. Stan Lee turned to John Romita to take over this important book. Oddly, John really didn't know anything about the popular web slinger. He stated, "My impression of Spider-Man was that this was a teenaged Clark Kent with glasses." He didn't expect to be working on it for long, just a temporary step-in. John always figured that Ditko would return. But that wasn't what happened.

John began his long-time work on Spider-Man in 1966. Each month, Stan would bring John a note telling the artist what evil character to use in the next month's issue. Together, John and Stan would work through the plot of the story, the setting, and the ending. In the beginning, it was a three-hour meeting, but after awhile, it only took an hour for them to develop the basics. Then it was up to John.

At first, Romita produced the comic book by keeping the Steve Ditko style. Thin lines filled the pages. The lead character, Peter Parker, was skinny and not too attractive. Over many years, however, John's great experience in romance comics helped him create his own Spider-Man style. Stan once told him that he was making Peter too handsome, too muscular. But that was John's style and that's how Peter "grew up."

Spider-Man, however, would not be the only popular comic book that Romita would work on. John was about to become "fantastic."

Below: Peter Parker meets the beautiful Mary Jane for the first time in *The Amazing Spider-Man #47*, April 1967, drawn by John Romita.

Above, left and right: The Amazing Spider-Man #108 & #109, May/June 1972, Romita's two favorite Spider-Man issues. John helped plot the stories and drew the villain in the style of Milton Caniff. Romita said, "Those two stories I'm proudest of as artwork."

Left and below: The Amazing Spider-Man #50, July 1967, cover and inside panel. Drawn by John Romita, it is one of the most famous issues ever created for Spider-Man.

Fantastic Four

When the amazing Marvel artist Jack Kirby left the company in 1970, he and Stan Lee's *Fantastic Four* comic book series was nearly 10 years old. Kirby had co-created and drawn the comic since its beginning in 1961. The popular superhero team featured four humans who had been showered with cosmic rays and possessed fantastic powers. Leader Reed Richards was "Mr. Fantastic," able to stretch like a rubber band. His future wife, Sue Storm, was "Invisible Woman." Johnny Storm could burst into flames and fly as "The Human Torch." Ben Grimm became the rock-like being known as "The Thing."

John Romita went in to Stan Lee's office when he found out that Jack had quit. John assumed that they would retire *Fantastic Four,* since it was really Kirby's book. Stan Lee gave him a different outcome: "You're going to do it!"

Again, John was given the task of keeping a style that wasn't his own. He mimicked Jack Kirby's *Fantastic Four,* and once said, "If it looked like me, it's only because I couldn't mimic him any better." But most people agreed that John kept the comic book going in the style they had come to know, and did a fantastic job of it.

Left: Line art of a *Fantastic Four* comic book page, drawn by John Romita.

Above and left: A collection of *Fantastic Four* covers created by John Romita. Artist Jack Kirby co-created and worked on the series for 10 years. After Kirby left Marvel, John picked up the series, creating a Kirby/Romita style.

Special Projects

John became art director at Marvel in the early 1970s in the Special Projects Department. One of his projects was creating *Spidey Super Stories*. These easy-to-read comic books were produced together with Public Broadcasting Service's young children's program, *The Electric Company*. Designed with basic page layouts and simple words, some 57 of these Spider-Man adventures were produced from October 1974 to March 1982. John Romita said, "We worked under the guidance of child psychologists to create these books. One of my proudest moments was receiving letters from teachers telling me how the Spidey books helped kids learn to read."

Another program John developed was for a little older group of "kids." Called "Romita's Raiders," this was an apprentice program for young artists just starting their careers.

The comic book business was often frantically busy. But at other times, there was little to do. Young artists were brought in to learn the business and to help out when needed. There wasn't much in the way of pay, but aspiring artists who showed promise could become one of Romita's Raiders. They got hands-on experience with comics and, when there was "down time," the young artists could work on their own projects. They had the chance to learn from some of the best artists in the business, including John Romita.

John helped, gave suggestions, encouraged, and basically created a place for new artists to grow. He wanted his students to be successful. Said John, "Not all well-trained artists will make it in comics. Just the ones who feel and care the most." John influenced these young people, as well as guiding one of his own.

Below: Spidey Super Stories #6, March 1975, cover art by John Romita.

Above: Self-portrait of John Romita, with several of his comic book characters.

In the Family

John and Virginia Romita had two sons: John, Jr., and Victor. Everyone in the Romita family was surrounded with Marvel characters. Since John, Sr., had so much work to do for Marvel, he often asked his family for story help. John, Sr., would say, "Stan wants me to do a certain thing, and I'm having trouble with this and that." Virginia, Victor, and John, Jr., all began throwing out ideas.

When John, Sr., had to draw Spider-Man's girlfriend, Mary Jane Watson, for the first time, he and Stan Lee were trying to decide if she would be beautiful or plain. John, Jr., had recently said to his father he thought that Peter Parker always had such bad luck. Based on his son's input, he gave Peter Parker a break and drew the famous Mary Jane as a "knockout."

Below: Virginia and John Romita, Sr. (standing), with Kathy and John Romita, Jr.

Surrounded by art and comics, it was no surprise that one of John and Virginia's kids grew up to become a comic book artist himself. John Romita, Jr., (who signs his work JRJR) followed in his dad's footsteps. He began working for Marvel in the 1970s. His first published work was a six-page backup story in *The Amazing Spider-Man Annual #4.* This led to work on such popular comic books as *The Uncanny X-Men, Iron Man*, and *Daredevil.*

Both father and son worked on *The Amazing Spider-Man,* including the web slinger's 500th issue, which was released in December 2003. The story featured a timeline of Spider-Man's past, and included pages penciled by both Romitas. John, Sr., is first to state that he is very proud of his son's unique art style and storytelling abilities.

Above: A small sampling of the work of comic book artist John Romita, Jr.

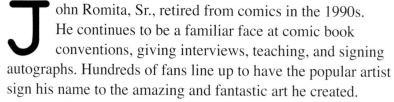

Still Helping People

John Romita, Sr., retired from comics in the 1990s. He continues to be a familiar face at comic book conventions, giving interviews, teaching, and signing autographs. Hundreds of fans line up to have the popular artist sign his name to the amazing and fantastic art he created.

In addition, John is a part of ACTOR, a non-profit corporation put together to help aging comic book creators. The name stands for "A Commitment To Our Roots." Many creators worked very hard for very little pay. Some now find themselves with no money and unable to work because of health problems.

John, Sr., along with several top comic industry leaders, raise money and give it to artists, writers, pencillers, inkers, colorists, and letterers who find themselves in need. John Romita, Sr., helped people all his life—young and old—and continues to do so today.

During much of his career, because John was younger than many of the top Marvel comic book artists, he often felt that he was trying to catch up. In fact, that was a time of learning. Wisely, he studied other artists' drawings in order to become better himself. Romita developed his own amazing talent, drawing beautiful faces and bodies of bold, yet clean, neat lines, and building a graphic story with his own unique flow and motion.

John has entertained and influenced millions of people. A grade school teacher once wrote to him to say that his work helped teach kids to read. Romita said that was one of his proudest moments.

Another Marvel artist, John Buscema, once found John erasing a page. When John didn't like something he'd drawn, he just couldn't continue working. Buscema told John to throw away the eraser, stating, "Stop erasing stuff you've drawn, because even your worst drawing is as good as anybody's best drawing." John Romita, Sr., worked hard to become one of the most loved and respected artists in the comic book business.

Above, left to right: Longtime Marvel associates, artist John Romita, inker Joe Sinnott, and writer/editor Stan Lee at a convention.

Glossary

BULLPEN

Members of the Marvel publishing staff, especially artists and writers.

CENSORSHIP

The control of what is written or spoken by a central authority, often a government or large group of outspoken individuals.

CO-CREATOR

A person working with another person to make up a comic book character. Especially in the comic book area, a writer and an artist often work together to develop a story, as well as a character's look, outfit, and special abilities.

COLORIST

The artist who adds color to a comic book page's finished black-and-white line art.

COMICS CODE AUTHORITY (CCA)

Established in 1954 as a way for comic book publishers to deal with parents' concerns about the effects of crime and horror comics on kids. Every comic book published required the CCA's seal of approval, and had to follow a strict set of guidelines. The Code is still in use today, although not all comic books are published with the CCA seal.

CREATOR

A person who thinks up the personality, physical look, and special skills of a comic book character.

DEADLINE
When a job or project must be completed. Usually an amount of time or specific date.

ILLUSTRATE
To add a piece of art to a printed story. The art may be a drawing, painting, or photo.

INKER
An artist who uses a pen or brush to apply black ink to roughly drawn ("penciled") comic book pages in order to create clean, clear lines.

JUVENILE DELINQUENCY

A juvenile is a young person, usually under the age of 18. Delinquency means acting antisocially, or breaking the law. In the mid-1950s, many people thought comic books that showed a lot of violence or antisocial behavior caused children to become juvenile delinquents. This debate is being argued again today, with violent video games taking the place of comic books.

KOREAN WAR
A civil war between North and South Korea that was fought from 1950 to 1953. The United States supported South Korea.

LETTERER
The person responsible for all the letters and words on a comic book page, including everything in word balloons, as well as sound effects.

PENCILLER
An artist who draws the rough pencil lines for comic book art.

SUPERHEROES
Characters, often human, but they may also be alien or mythological beings, who develop or have special skills that give them superhuman powers. These characters use their powers for good, helping and protecting people.

Index

A

Action Comics #1 4
ACTOR (A Commitment To Our Roots) 28
Air Force, U.S. 10
Amazing Spider-Man, The 4, 26
Amazing Spider-Man Annual #4 26
Atlas Comics 8, 11
Avengers, The 18

B

Batman 19
Brooklyn, NY 4
Buscema, John 29

C

Caniff, Milton 6
Captain America 4, 6
Coca-Cola 8
Collier's Weekly 8
Comics Code Authority (CCA) 13
Comics Magazine Association of America 13

D

Daredevil, The Man Without Fear 4, 19, 26
DC Comics 11, 15, 16, 18, 19
Ditko, Steve 20

E

Electric Company, The 24

Empire State Building 9
Everett, Bill 19

F

Falling in Love 16
Fantastic Four 4, 22
Fantastic, Mr. 22
First Amendment 13

G

Girls' Love Stories 16
Goodman, Martin 15
Governor's Island 10, 11
Grimm, Ben 22

H

Human Torch, The 22

I

Infantino, Carmine 11, 16
Infantino, Jimmy 11
Invisible Woman 22
Iron Man 26

K

Kent, Clark 20
Kirby, Jack 6, 19, 22
Korean War 9, 10, 11

L

Lee, Stan 8, 9, 10, 11, 15, 17, 18, 19, 20, 22, 26

M

Marvel Comics 8, 15, 17, 18, 19, 20, 22, 24, 26, 28, 29

Metamorpho 19
Murdock, Matthew Michael 19

N

New York, NY 6
New York Harbor 10
New York Public Library 9
North Korea 10

P

Parker, Peter 20, 26
Public Broadcasting Service (PBS) 24

R

Richards, Reed 22
Romita, John Jr. 26
Romita, John Sr. 4, 6, 8, 9, 10, 11, 12, 15, 16, 17, 18, 19, 20, 22, 24, 26, 28, 29
Romita, Marie 4
Romita, Victor (father) 4
Romita, Victor (son) 11, 26
Romita, Virginia 9, 11, 12, 26
Romita's Raiders 24

S

Saturday Evening Post 8
School of Industrial Art (SIA) 6, 8
seal of approval 13
Secret Hearts 16
Senate Judiciary Committee 12

South Korea 10
Special Projects Department 24
Spider-Man 20, 24, 26
Spidey Super Stories 24
Statue of Liberty 6
Storm, Johnny 22
Storm, Sue 22
Superman 4, 19

T

Terry and the Pirates 6
Thing, The 22
Timely Comics 8, 9, 10, 11

U

United States 10

W

Watson, Mary Jane 26

X

X-Men, The Uncanny 26

Z

Zakarin, Lester 8, 10